CREATURES
OF THE NIGHT

AYE-AYES

QUINN M. ARNOLD

CREATIVE EDUCATION • CREATIVE PAPERBACKS

CONTENTS

NIGHT FALLS OVER A FOREST IN MADAGASCAR. HIGH
IN THE CANOPY, AN AYE-AYE POKES ITS HEAD OUT

OF A BALL-SHAPED NEST. IT SNIFFS THE AIR. EXITING THE NEST, IT CLIMBS ALONG A BRANCH, LOOKING FOR FOOD.

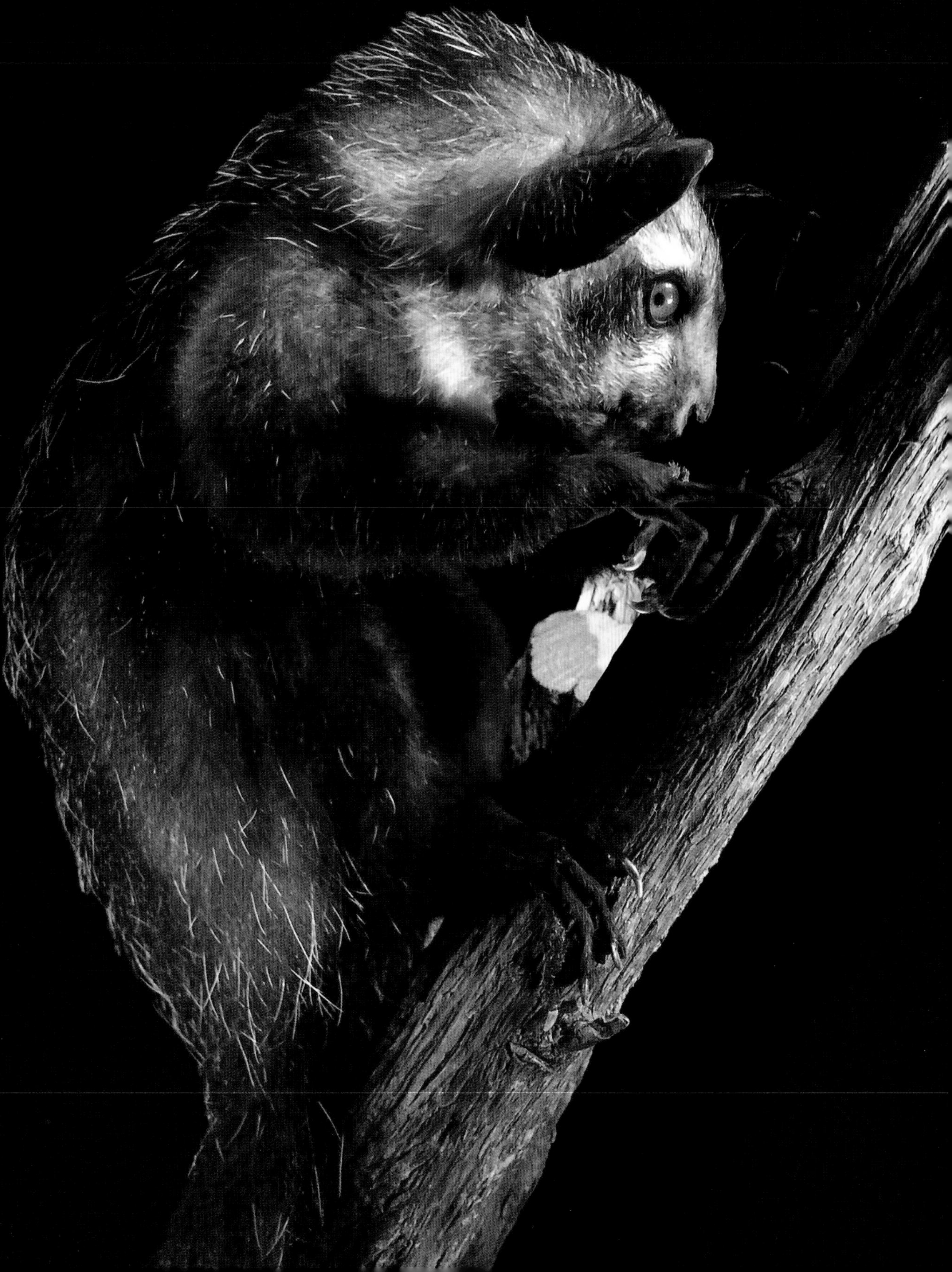

AYE-AYES ARE FOUND
ONLY IN MADAGASCAR.

Aye-ayes are lemurs. They are **nocturnal**. These tree-dwelling creatures weigh only five pounds (2.3 kg). Yet they are the world's largest nocturnal **primates**.

GREEN EYES AT BIRTH TURN GOLDEN-YELLOW | CAN SEE IN COLOR | 80% OF THE NIGHT SPENT TRAVELING AND LOOKING FOR FOOD |

Aye-ayes are 12 to 16 inches (30.5–40.6 cm) long. Their bushy tails are longer than their bodies. Dark, shaggy hair helps aye-ayes blend into the night.

The aye-aye's round, golden-yellow eyes gleam in dim light. This is called eyeshine. It helps animals see in the dark. A see-through inner eyelid keeps aye-aye eyes clean and moist.

A

ye-ayes are **forage** feeders. They travel up to two miles (3.2 km) each night as they look for food. Aye-ayes eat eggs, fruits, and nuts. Sometimes they **raid** coconut or mango farms. But their favorite food is **larvae**.

AYE-AYE DIET

RAMY NUTS

LARVAE

FRUIT

An aye-aye taps a tree with its sensitive middle finger. It tilts its large ears. It listens carefully. When it finds larvae, the aye-aye gnaws through the bark with its sharp front teeth. Then it sticks its long, thin finger into the larval tunnel. It hooks larvae with its claw.

AYE-AYE HAND

Baby aye-ayes drink milk from their mothers. Their mothers teach them how to tap-forage. They stop drinking milk around seven months of age.

LIFE OF AN AYE-AYE

BIRTH
green eyes; weighs 4 oz (113 g)

2 MONTHS
floppy ears stiffen; leaves nest

7 MONTHS
loses baby teeth; stops drinking milk

2 YEARS
leaves mother to live alone

3–4 YEARS
weighs 5 lbs (2.3 kg); reproduces

10–20 YEARS
end of life

Older aye-ayes live alone. Each one has a home range. These areas often overlap. Aye-ayes scent-mark their boundaries. They sniff the branches for these scents. This helps them avoid each other.

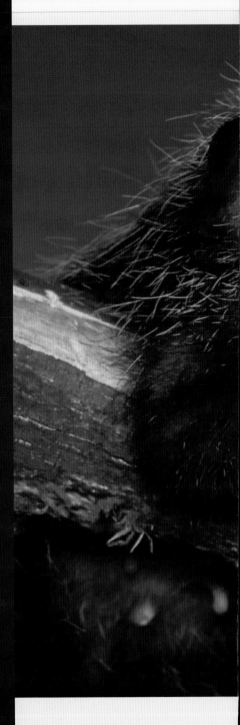

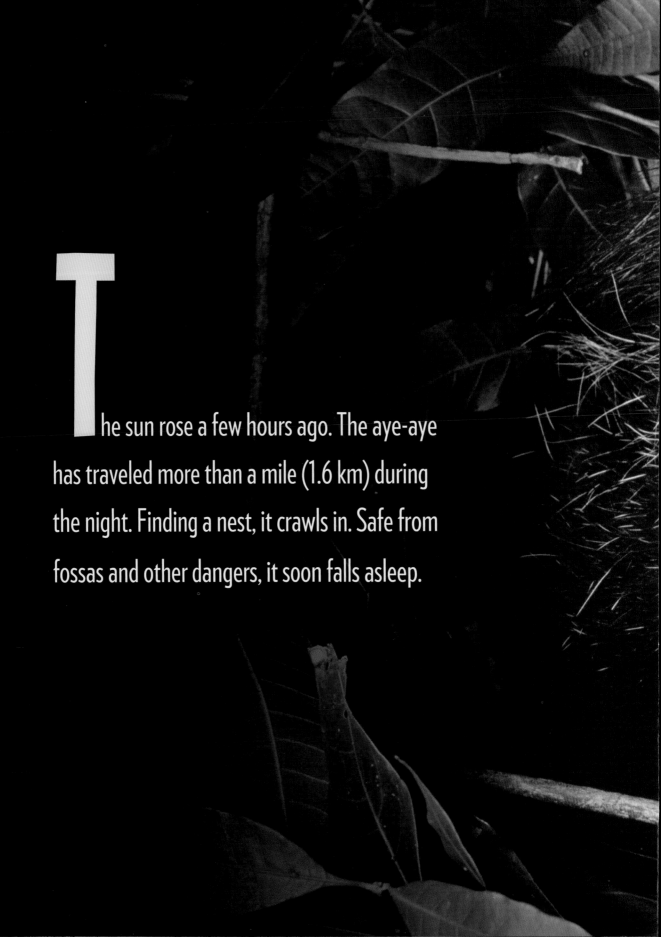

The sun rose a few hours ago. The aye-aye has traveled more than a mile (1.6 km) during the night. Finding a nest, it crawls in. Safe from fossas and other dangers, it soon falls asleep.

EARS

ridges in hairless ears
enhance sounds; ears are
about 4 inches (10.2 cm) long
and 2.5 inches (6.4 cm) wide

SNOUT >

slit-shaped nostrils
improve excellent
sense of smell

TEETH

front teeth (incisors)
never stop growing

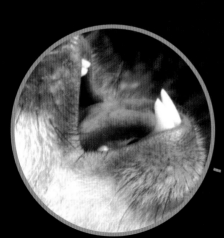

FINGERS

middle digit is longer and slimmer than other fingers

TAIL

20 to 22 inches (50.8–55.9 cm) long; hair on tail is about 9 inches (22.9 cm) long

CLAWS

sharply pointed to grab branches and nab larvae

GLOSSARY

CANOPY
the uppermost branches of trees in a forest

LARVAE
the newly hatched, often wormlike form of many insects

PRIMATES
mammals (animals with hair or fur that feed their babies milk) with gripping hands and a large brain; most primates live in trees

FORAGE
to search widely for food

NOCTURNAL
active at night

RAID
to steal goods

READ MORE

Bédoyère, Camilla de la. *Creatures of the Night*. Buffalo, N.Y.: Firefly Books, 2014.

Bluemel Oldfield, Dawn. *Aye-aye*. New York: Bearport, 2018.

Owings, Lisa. *Aye-aye*. Minneapolis: Bellwether Media, 2014.

WEBSITES

Active Wild: Aye-Aye Facts
https://www.activewild.com/aye-aye-facts/

Duke Lemur Center: Aye-Aye
https://lemur.duke.edu/discover/meet-the-lemurs/aye-aye/

National Geographic Kids: Aye-aye
https://kids.nationalgeographic.com/animals/aye-aye/

Note: Every effort has been made to ensure that the websites listed above are suitable for children, that they have educational value, and that they contain no inappropriate material. However, because of the nature of the Internet, it is impossible to guarantee that these sites will remain active indefinitely or that their contents will not be altered.

INDEX

PUBLISHED BY CREATIVE EDUCATION AND CREATIVE PAPERBACKS

P.O. Box 227, Mankato, Minnesota 56002
Creative Education and Creative Paperbacks
are imprints of The Creative Company
www.thecreativecompany.us

LIBRARY OF CONGRESS CATALOGING-IN-PUBLICATION DATA

Names: Arnold, Quinn M., author.
Title: Aye-ayes / Quinn M. Arnold.
Series: Creatures of the night.
Includes index.
Summary: Peer into the nocturnal Madagascan forest canopies with this high-interest introduction to the long-fingered primates known as aye-ayes.

Identifiers:
LCCN: 2018059115
ISBN 978-1-64026-116-7 (hardcover)
ISBN 978-1-62832-679-6 (pbk)
ISBN 978-1-64000-234-0 (eBook)

Subjects: LCSH: Aye-aye—Juvenile literature.
Nocturnal animals—Juvenile literature.
Classification: LCC QL737.P935 A77 2019 / DDC 599.8/3—dc23

CCSS: RI.1.1-6; RI.2.1-7; RF.1.1-4; RF.2.1-4

DESIGN AND PRODUCTION

by Joe Kahnke; art direction by Rita Marshall
Printed in China

PHOTOGRAPHS by Alamy (A & J Visage, Paul Bolotov, Gabbro, Chris Hellier, National Geographic Image Collection, RGB Ventures/SuperStock), Getty Images (Mark Carwardine/Photolibrary, David Haring/DUPC/Oxford Scientific, Mint Images - Frans Lanting, Oxford Scientific/Photolibrary), iStockphoto (dennisvdw), Minden Pictures (Pete Oxford), Shutterstock (Anatolir, Dzm1try, Stephen Marques, MegSopki, Melin Creative, Anna Veselova)

Image on page 14 courtesy of Denver Zoo.

FIRST EDITION HC 9 8 7 6 5 4 3 2 1
FIRST EDITION PBK 9 8 7 6 5 4 3 2 1